B1 PRELIMINARY 1

WITHOUT ANSWERS

AUTHENTIC PRACTICE TESTS

Cambridge University Press
www.cambridge.org/elt

Cambridge Assessment English
www.cambridgeenglish.org

Information on this title: www.cambridge.org/9781108723688

© Cambridge University Press and UCLES 2019

It is normally necessary for written permission for copying to be obtained *in advance* from a publisher. The sample answer sheets at the back of this book are designed to be copied and distributed in class.
The normal requirements are waived here and it is not necessary to write to Cambridge University Press for permission for an individual teacher to make copies for use within his or her own classroom. Only those pages that carry the wording '© UCLES 2019 Photocopiable' may be copied.

First published 2019

20 19 18 17 16 15 14 13 12 11 10 9 8 7 6

Printed in Great Britain by CPI Group (UK) Ltd, Croydon CR0 4YY

A catalogue record for this publication is available from the British Library

ISBN 978-1-108-67641-0 Preliminary 1 Student's Book with answers with Audio
ISBN 978-1-108-72368-8 Preliminary 1 Student's Book without answers
ISBN 978-1-108-72369-5 Audio CDs (2)

The publishers have no responsibility for the persistence or accuracy of URLs for external or third-party internet websites referred to in this publication, and do not guarantee that any content on such websites is, or will remain, accurate or appropriate. Information regarding prices, travel timetables, and other factual information given in this work is correct at the time of first printing but the publishers do not guarantee the accuracy of such information thereafter.

Contents

Introduction		5
Speaking: an overview for candidates		7
Test 1	Reading	8
	Writing	18
	Listening	20
Test 2	Reading	26
	Writing	36
	Listening	38
Test 3	Reading	44
	Writing	54
	Listening	56
Test 4	Reading	62
	Writing	72
	Listening	74
Sample answer sheets		80
Acknowledgements		85
Visual materials for the Speaking test		86

Introduction

This collection of four complete practice tests contains papers from the *Cambridge English Qualifications B1 Preliminary* examination. Students can practise these tests on their own or with the help of a teacher.

The *B1 Preliminary* examination is part of a series of Cambridge English Qualifications for general and higher education. This series consists of five qualifications that have similar characteristics but are designed for different levels of English language ability. The *B1 Preliminary* certificate is recognised around the world as proof of intermediate level English skills for industrial, administrative and service-based employment. It is also accepted by a wide range of educational institutions for study purposes.

Cambridge English Qualifications	CEFR Level	UK National Qualifications Framework Level
C2 Proficiency	C2	3
C1 Advanced	C1	2
B2 First	B2	1
B1 Preliminary	B1	Entry 3
A2 Key	A2	Entry 2

Further information

The information contained in this practice book is designed to be an overview of the exam. For a full description of all of the above exams, including information about task types, testing focus and preparation, please see the relevant handbooks which can be obtained from the Cambridge Assessment English website at: **cambridgeenglish.org**.

The structure of *B1 Preliminary*: an overview

The *Cambridge English Qualifications B1 Preliminary* examination consists of four papers:

Reading: 45 minutes
Candidates need to be able to understand the main points from signs, newspapers and magazines and use vocabulary and structures correctly.

Writing: 45 minutes
Candidates need to be able to respond to an email and to write either an article or a story.

Listening: 30 minutes approximately (plus 6 minutes to transfer answers)
Candidates need to show they can follow and understand a range of spoken materials including announcements and discussions about everyday life.

Speaking: 10–12 minutes (or 15–17 minutes for groups of 3)
Candidates take the Speaking test with another candidate or in a group of three. They are tested on their ability to take part in different types of interaction: with the examiner, with the other candidate and by themselves.

	Overall length	Number of tasks/parts	Number of items
Reading	45 mins	6	32
Writing	45 mins	2	–
Listening	approx. 30 mins	4	25
Speaking	10–12 mins	4	–
Total	approx. 2 hours 10 mins		

Grading

All candidates receive a Statement of Results and candidates whose performance ranges between CEFR Levels A2 and B2 (Cambridge English Scale scores of 120–170) also receive a certificate.

- Candidates who achieve **Grade A** (Cambridge English Scale scores of 160–170) receive the Preliminary English Test certificate stating that they demonstrated ability at Level B2.

- Candidates who achieve **Grade B** or **C** (Cambridge English Scale scores of 140–159) receive the Preliminary English Test certificate at Level B1.

- Candidates whose performance is below A2 level, but falls within **Level A2** (Cambridge English Scale scores of 120–139), receive a Cambridge English certificate stating that they have demonstrated ability at Level A2.

For further information on grading and results, go to the website (see page 5 for details).

Speaking: an overview for candidates

The Speaking test lasts 10–12 minutes (or 15–17 minutes for groups of 3). You will take the test with another candidate. There are two examiners but only one of them will talk to you. The examiner will ask you questions and ask you to talk to the other candidate.

Part 1 (2–3 minutes)
The examiner will ask you and your partner some questions in turn. These questions will be about your personal details, daily routines, likes, dislikes, etc. You will only speak to the examiner in this part.

Part 2 (2–3 minutes)
The examiner will give you a colour photograph to talk about. The photograph will show an everyday situation. You will be given one minute to describe what you can see in the photograph.

Part 3 (3 minutes)
In this part, you and your partner will talk to each other. The examiner will give you a card with some illustrations on it that are connected to an imaginary situation. You will then be given about two minutes to discuss ideas with your partner. During the discussion, you should make and respond to suggestions, discuss alternatives, make recommendations and negotiate agreement with your partner.

Part 4 (3 minutes)
The examiner will ask you and your partner some questions about the topic introduced in Part 3. The questions will focus on your likes, dislikes, habits and opinions. The examiner will either ask you to respond individually to the questions, or to discuss them with your partner.

Test 1

READING (45 minutes)

Part 1

Questions 1–5

For each question, choose the correct answer.

1

College Shop
Now is the time to buy essential items like pens and folders – prices reduced until Friday.
Open daily during lunch breaks. Also for 30 minutes after last class everyday apart from Monday.

A Students must go to the college shop to buy certain items for their studies.

B Students can take advantage of special offers at the college shop at the moment.

C Students may visit the college shop at lunchtime every day except Monday.

2

Hi Max
I'm afraid I'll no longer be able to come on the shopping trip tomorrow. My aunt is visiting and didn't give us much notice.
Jake

Jake is writing to

A suggest a new date for a shopping trip.

B invite Max to meet one of his relatives.

C cancel an arrangement he had made.

3

Special Offer

Order any pizza by 7 p.m. and get another one half-price!

A All the pizzas in the restaurant are included in this offer.

B Any pizza ordered before 7 p.m. costs less than the usual price.

C At certain times, a customer can get two pizzas for the price of one.

4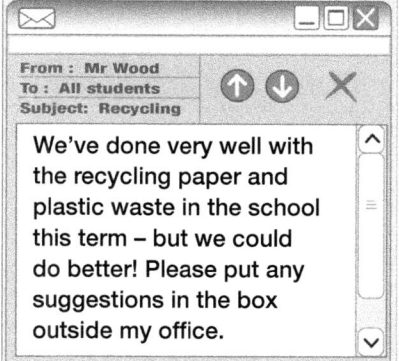

A Mr Wood has made suggestions on how to recycle waste produced by the school.

B Recycling materials should be put into the box outside Mr Wood's office.

C Mr Wood wants new ideas on ways to improve waste recycling in the school.

5

Mel is texting to

A accept Sam's invitation to the cinema.

B admit to Sam that she found the film scary.

C ask when Sam can see another film with her.

Part 2

Questions 6–10

For each question, choose the correct answer.

The people below all want to find a book to read.
On the opposite page there are eight book reviews.
Decide which book would be the most suitable for the people below.

6  Ahmed enjoys reading about real people, especially if they tell their own story. He'd like to read a book by someone who's had to deal with difficulties in their life.

7  Pritti loves doing all kinds of sport. She'd like to learn as much as possible about top sportspeople from all over the world and how they've managed to achieve their goals.

8  Conal loves nature and enjoys writing about it. He wants ideas to help him further develop his writing skills and would love to have a career as a writer.

9  Elif likes reading books about adventures. She loves learning about people who did brave things in the past, and how their actions have influenced the way we live today.

10  Stefan enjoys travelling and is keen to discover more about other cultures. He also wants to learn how to make typical dishes from a variety of countries.

Book reviews

A Being Me
This book is full of practical advice for anyone who wants to be fit and healthy. Famous sportspeople have contributed their favourite recipes, and you'll also find instructions for a daily exercise routine.

B Endless Days
In this book, the novelist tells the true story of the first pilots to fly across the Atlantic. With plenty of photographs and a detailed discussion of the importance of these events for the modern world, the book successfully brings history to life for readers everywhere.

C Action Plan
Action Plan is all about famous athletes, and there are some amazing photos of them competing. There are also lots of interviews about what they've done to succeed in their careers. You'll find out about things like the food they eat, the number of hours they train, and what they do to prepare for important competitions.

D Memories
The prize-winning author of *Memories* is famous for his unusual writing style and exciting adventure stories. In this book, he takes us on a journey around the world and teaches us a lot about other cultures and their histories. He describes some of the world's most beautiful nature, as well as the many interesting people he has met.

E Days in the Sun
In this book, a well-known author describes his happy early life growing up on a small Irish farm and how travelling around the countryside inspired him to become an author. He describes in detail how he improved his style, and his experiences will interest anyone who is hoping to get their own work published.

F Parrots in Paradise
This newly published adventure story is about a young girl who's lost on a beautiful island with only birds and animals for company. The story deals with some of the difficulties she has, but there's also lots of excitement. If you love well-written fiction, this book's for you!

G Night Light
In *Night Light*, the writer tells us how he became a world-class athlete. He talks about his life as a blind person, and describes the challenges he faced on his way to the top in the world of sports. The book is written in an entertaining and amusing style, which makes it a very enjoyable read.

H *Our Lives*
This is the perfect book if you're interested in how people live in different parts of the world. It also includes recipes for traditional meals from these places. There are wonderful photos, not only of the people, but also of the wildlife and scenery in each location.

Part 3

Questions 11–15

For each question, choose the correct answer.

Cyclist Vicky Harmiston

Reporter Mark Lewis writes about Vicky Harmiston, who has had a successful career as a track cyclist – a cyclist who races on special race tracks.

When Vicky Harmiston was a child, her parents gave her and her brother Jamie the freedom to decide what they did in their spare time. Vicky chose to do lots of different sports. She was a good swimmer, and the coach at the swimming club she went to thought she might be good enough to become a champion. But the club was a long way from her home so it was difficult for her to fit in the training around her schoolwork. When they were teenagers, Jamie, who loved cycling, bought himself a special track-racing bike and started taking part in competitions. Vicky thought it looked very exciting and decided to try it for herself. She says that was the best decision she ever made. Soon she was cycling every day and doing really well. The track was near her school, which meant it was no problem for her to attend training sessions after school every day.

Vicky went on to have a successful career in track cycling and won several competitions. Then, when she was 28, she retired from competitive cycling. Vicky told me: 'For years I'd loved winning competitions but I began to get a bit tired of the whole thing – and when the excitement stops, there's no point. Luckily, I went on to have a new career.'

Vicky got a job with a charity called CycleZone. 'We work with young people who have never enjoyed sport,' she says. 'The first thing we do is teach them to ride a bike. We want them to learn to believe in themselves and their own abilities. CycleZone does a great job, and it gets young people together so they're part of a wider group.'

The charity uses celebrities to advertise the work they do. Vicky says, 'I know some people aren't sure whether the support of a celebrity is always positive for a charity. They say the celebrities are only doing it to push themselves forward, which prevents the public from seeing the real work of the charity. But if famous singers and actors, for example, can help, I think they should.'

Reading

11   When Vicky first started cycling

   A   she had a very good coach.

   B   her parents gave her helpful advice.

   C   she could get to a race track easily.

   D   her brother gave her a great bike.

12   Why does Vicky say she stopped cycle racing?

   A   She felt she was too old to do it.

   B   She was becoming bored with it.

   C   She had won everything she wanted.

   D   She was preparing for a new career.

13   What does the charity CycleZone do for young people?

   A   It teaches them how to do track racing.

   B   It supports those who have talent.

   C   It offers them the chance to try a variety of sports.

   D   It helps them become more confident.

14   According to Vicky, some people believe that celebrities can

   A   take attention away from what a charity does.

   B   help people understand a charity's work.

   C   make the public care less about a charity.

   D   encourage more people to become involved with a charity.

15   What would Vicky say on her blog?

   A   As a child, I always knew what I wanted to do when I grew up. But I never expected to become so famous.

   B   If you join CycleZone, you'll get to meet celebrities and learn how they've become successful.

   C   Although track cycling is not the only sport I've been good at, I've never regretted my choice of career.

   D   In my spare time I love going to schools and helping groups of children learn to ride bikes.

Part 4

Questions 16–20

Five sentences have been removed from the text below.
For each question, choose the correct answer.
There are three extra sentences which you do not need to use.

At home together

Taimi Taskinen is an 83-year-old woman who lives in a care home called Rudolf House in Helsinki, Finland. A care home is a place where old people can live and be looked after if they don't live with their families. At Rudolf House, there are lots of stairs, so there are some rooms which elderly people can't access easily. As a result, the city council decided to rent these spare rooms to young people. They called this new housing programme 'The House that Fits'.

When Taimi heard about the council's plan, she wondered how it was going to work. **16** [ ] She couldn't imagine what she'd have in common with young people who weren't family members. Then, one morning a few days later, a young man appeared outside her room. **17** [ ]

'Hi! I'm your new neighbour,' the young man said. 'My name's Jonatan Shaya. Mind if I come in?' 'Please do,' she replied, immediately curious. 'I'll make coffee,' he announced, going into her tiny kitchen. 'Why don't you tell me about yourself?' he asked, as he brought their drinks to the table.

18 [ ] She also told him about her family and how much she loved making art.

In turn, 20-year-old Jonatan told Taimi he'd been living in Helsinki with his mother and younger brother until they moved away. He was in the middle of a course in the city, training to become a chef. **19** [ ] That's when he heard about 'The House that Fits' on social media. The council's post resulted in over 300 young people applying to live at Rudolf House. They had face-to-face interviews and wrote short essays about why they wanted to live there. **20** [ ] And that's how the unlikely friendship between Taimi and Jonatan began.

A	Surprising herself, she talked about growing up in a lakeside town in eastern Finland.
B	Therefore, he needed to find somewhere to live.
C	As a result, she wasn't sure whether the young people had arrived.
D	She'd left the door open, as she always did in the morning.
E	In the end, three of them, including Jonatan, were chosen.
F	Because of this, Jonatan has to be a good neighbour and spend 30 hours a month with Taimi.
G	It would be the first time that anything like this had happened at Rudolf House.
H	Instead, they just talked, as if they'd known each other forever.

Test 1

Part 5

Questions 21–26

For each question, choose the correct answer.

The invention of crisps

Potato crisps were invented by accident in 1853, by a chef called George Crum. He was extremely **(21)** .... of his cookery skills, and the expensive hotel where he worked attracted customers who were **(22)** .... to eating only the best food.

One evening, a particularly difficult-to-please guest complained about Crum's fried potatoes. 'They're too thick,' he said, 'too soft, and have no flavour.' He **(23)** .... that they should be replaced.

The customer's negative **(24)** .... made Crum extremely angry, so he decided to annoy the customer. He cut a potato into paper-thin slices, fried the pieces until they were hard, then put far too much salt on them. 'He'll hate them,' Crum thought. But the customer loved them and ordered more.

News of this new snack travelled fast and an absolutely **(25)** .... global industry has grown from Crum's invention – even though his fried potatoes were actually **(26)** .... to taste disgusting!

21	A	proud	B	satisfied	C	pleased	D	impressed
22	A	prepared	B	familiar	C	used	D	known
23	A	convinced	B	wanted	C	needed	D	demanded
24	A	comments	B	notes	C	reasons	D	explanations
25	A	big	B	huge	C	large	D	wide
26	A	hoped	B	intended	C	attempted	D	tried

Part 6

Questions 27–32

For each question, write the correct answer.
Write **one** word for each gap.

Moving house

Hi Alex,

How are you? This week's been a very busy one for me – I finally moved house! **(27)** .... wasn't until I started to pack a few days ago that I realised how much stuff I had. I really think moving house is one of the **(28)** .... stressful things I've ever done! I was sad to leave my old house – after **(29)** ...., I'd lived there my whole life so I have lots of good memories.

Anyway, I'm looking **(30)** .... to being in this new house. It's not as big as the old one, but **(31)** .... least it's got a great garden. I'm planning to have a small party on Saturday night. Are you free then? Why don't you come along **(32)** .... you are? I hope you can make it. Let me know.

All the best,

Sam

Test 1

WRITING (45 minutes)

Part 1

You **must** answer this question.
Write your answer in about **100 words** on the answer sheet.

Question 1

Read this email from your English-speaking college classmate Alex and the notes you have made.

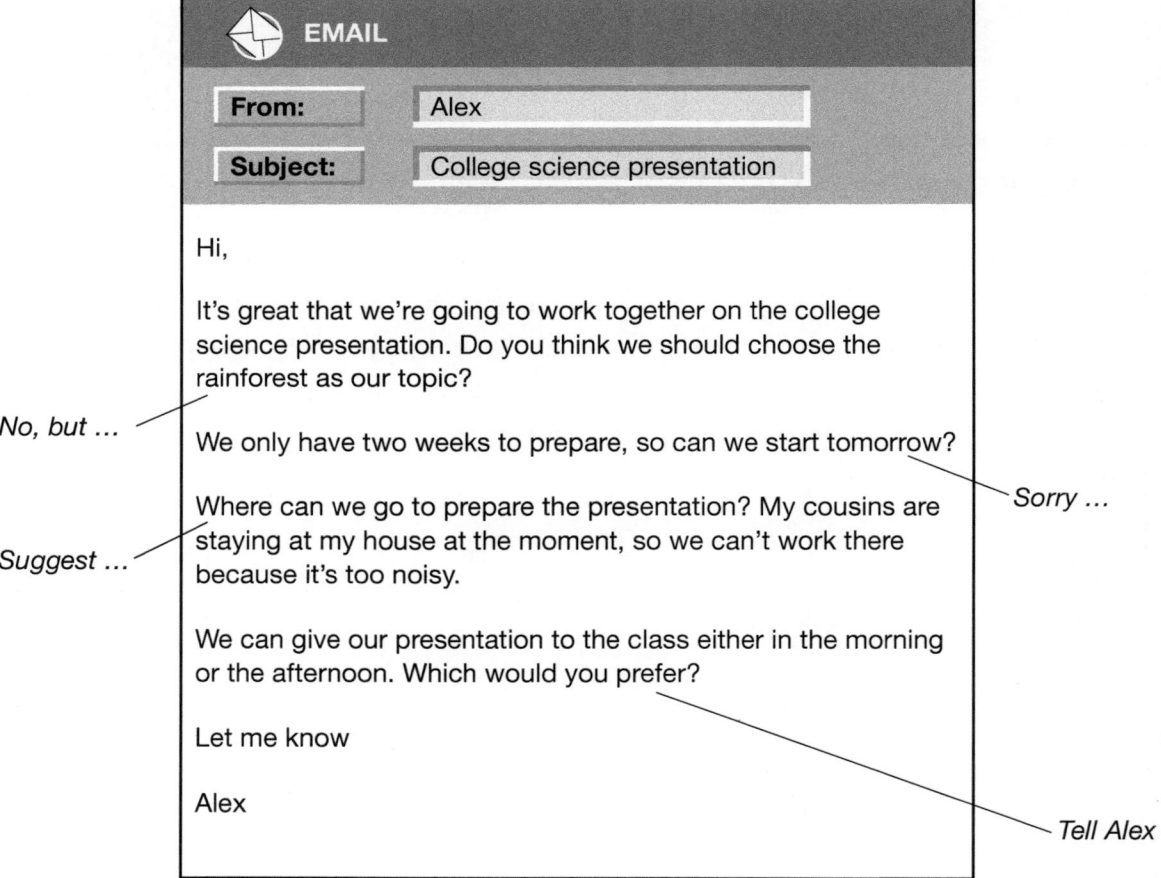

Write your **email** to Alex using **all the notes**.

18

Part 2

Choose **one** of these questions.
Write your answer in about **100 words** on the answer sheet.

Question 2

You see this announcement in an English-language magazine.

Articles wanted!
Is shopping boring? What do you like and dislike about shopping? What could shopping centres do to attract more people? Write us an article answering these questions. The best one will win a prize!

Write your **article**.

Question 3

Your English teacher has asked you to write a story.
Your story must begin with this sentence.

Jack climbed out of the boat and ran as fast as he could to the beach.

Write your **story**.

Test 1

LISTENING (approximately 30 minutes)

Part 1

Questions 1–7

For each question, choose the correct answer.

---

1 Where does the man think he left his wallet?

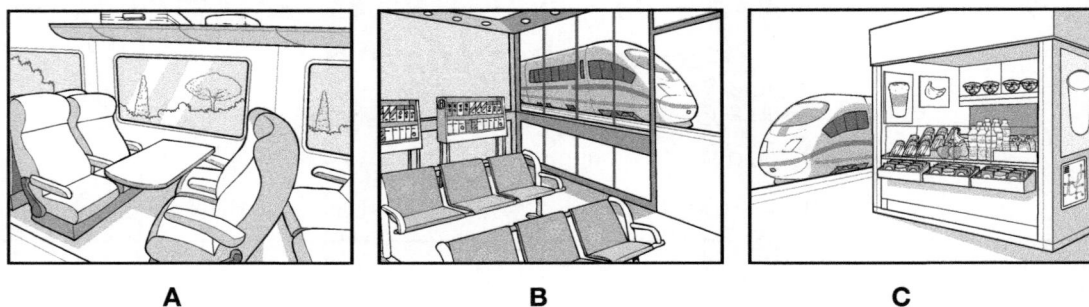

A   B   C

2 What is tomorrow's talk at the Nature Society about?

A   B   C

3 What will the woman order for lunch?

A   B   C

Listening

4 How did the woman find out about the exhibition?

A B C

5 What is the woman's brother doing?

A B C

6 How will the woman travel to her meeting?

A B C

7 Which sport has the man stopped doing?

A B C

Test 1

Part 2

Questions 8–13

For each question, choose the correct answer.

---

8   You will hear two people talking about buying a bicycle.
    The woman suggests that the man should

    A   try looking online.

    B   go to a different shop.

    C   get advice from an expert.

9   You will hear a man telling his friend about his Welsh language course.
    What does the man say about it?

    A   The teacher speaks too fast.

    B   The lessons are too long.

    C   The grammar is too difficult.

10 You will hear a woman telling her colleague about her weekend.
    What did the woman like about it?

    A   visiting a new place in the city

    B   seeing her children enjoying themselves

    C   having a chance to relax

11 You will hear two friends talking about a new restaurant.
    They both think the restaurant would be better if

    A   the food was fresher.

    B   the service was faster.

    C   the prices were cheaper.

Listening

12 You will hear two old friends talking at a party.
How is the man's appearance different from before?

- **A** He has grown a beard.
- **B** He has started wearing glasses.
- **C** He has changed his style of clothes.

13 You will hear two colleagues talking about a meeting.
How does the woman feel about it?

- **A** annoyed that she will have to attend it
- **B** worried that her presentation will be unpopular
- **C** surprised that it is still going to take place

Test 1

Part 3

Questions 14–19

For each question, write the correct answer in the gap. Write **one** or **two words** or a **number** or a **date** or a **time**.

You will hear a man giving information to people who are starting a one-week singing course.

One-week singing course

Teachers

Jazz: Robert Park

Songs from musicals: **(14)** Susan ....

Concert

When: Friday, at **(15)** .... p.m.

Colour of clothes: **(16)** ....

Other general information

Map of building: available from the **(17)** ....

Lunch: eat in the **(18)** ....

Car park: costs £ **(19)** .... per day

Part 4

Questions 20–25

For each question, choose the correct answer.

You will hear an interview with a man called Mickey Diaz, who is talking about his work as a hairdresser.

20 Why did Mickey decide to become a hairdresser?

    A   He was offered a job by a friend.

    B   He wanted to do what his family did.

    C   He hoped to meet some famous people.

21 On a typical day at work, Mickey says that he

    A   doesn't take enough time for breaks.

    B   works longer hours than he would like to.

    C   tries to do a range of jobs.

22 The part of the job which Mickey likes most is

    A   creating new haircuts.

    B   hearing about customers' lives.

    C   using his imagination.

23 What part of his job does Mickey dislike?

    A   having to do boring courses

    B   sharing ideas with colleagues

    C   dealing with difficult customers

24 How does Mickey feel after cutting a customer's hair?

    A   worried that the customer may be annoyed.

    B   proud of what he's achieved.

    C   keen to continue learning.

25 Mickey recommends that people who want to work as hairdressers

    A   shouldn't take the first job they're offered.

    B   shouldn't believe they know everything.

    C   shouldn't expect to earn much at first.

Test 2

READING (45 minutes)

Part 1

Questions 1–5

For each question, choose the correct answer.

1

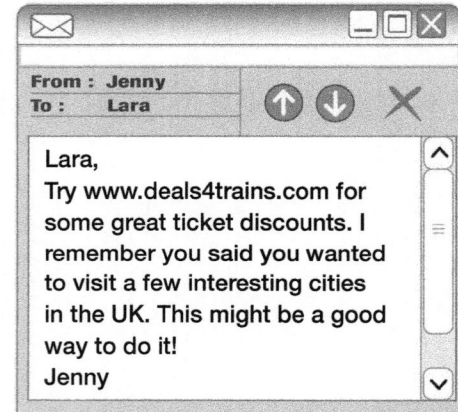

Jenny is emailing to

A suggest how Lara could do some sightseeing.

B remind Lara that she needs to book some cheap train tickets.

C invite Lara to visit some different places around the UK with her.

2

A People will be asked to discuss their favourite childhood sweets at the lecture.

B The lecture will be about how sweet shops have changed over the last century.

C The lecture will cover some surprising facts about sweets.

3

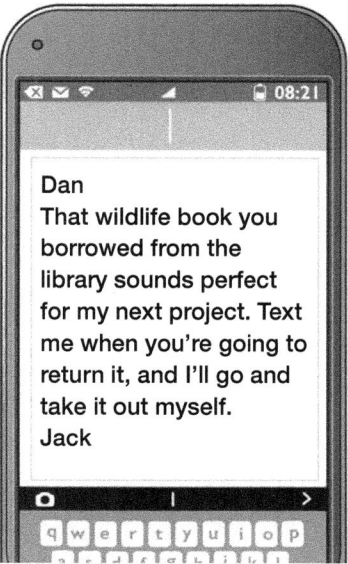

Dan
That wildlife book you borrowed from the library sounds perfect for my next project. Text me when you're going to return it, and I'll go and take it out myself.
Jack

A Jack is asking Dan's opinion about whether a book is suitable for his project.

B Jack wants Dan to let him know when a library book will be available.

C Jack is recommending to Dan a useful library book he has recently borrowed.

4

Tomato sauce
Store in cool, dry place. After opening, keep in fridge and use within six weeks, and not after date shown.

A Eat the sauce a maximum of six weeks after you start using it.

B Put the sauce in your refrigerator as soon as you bring it home.

C Make a note of the date when you bought the sauce.

5

DRUM TUTOR

All abilities & styles covered

Adults only (18+)

First lesson costs absolutely nothing when signing up for two months!

A The teacher is offering lessons to anyone interested in trying the drums.

B You must intend to study for a certain period to have the free session.

C To attend these classes, students must already be at a certain level.

Part 2

Questions 6–10

For each question, choose the correct answer.

The young people below are all interested in protecting the environment.
On the opposite page there are descriptions of eight websites on the environment.
Decide which website would be the most suitable for the people below.

6  Ethan wants to know about environmental organisations around the world. He's interested in doing a project at home on energy production, and wants recommendations for other websites with up-to-date information on new research.

7  Mario is interested in how the way he gets to work affects the environment, and wants ideas to reduce any negative effects. He'd like to meet local people who share his interest in the environment.

8  Sylvia is keen to know what she can do with items she doesn't need, rather than throw them away. She'd like the opportunity to ask environmental experts about their work.

9  Declan wants to know where to find clothes produced without damaging the environment. He'd like to learn about recycling processes, and see how recycling is done internationally.

10  Tasha wants to help her family save energy, and get a basic introduction to studying the environment for a college project. She'd also like to buy something created from recycled items.

Websites on the environment

A futurenow.org
Find answers here about how much energy is used around the planet. And if you're planning a journey, put in your route to compare the energy used by different types of transport, and choose the one that's best for the environment.

B ourworld.org
This site lists the best places online to learn the latest results of scientific studies on issues affecting the environment. Or if you prefer working things out for yourself, there are experiments to do like making your own power using sunlight! You'll also find information on groups all over the planet working to protect the environment.

C cleanplanet.org
Discover how waste plastic, glass and metal are turned into new products, and watch clips showing different methods used around the world. There's also a section about how much attention various fashion companies pay to their effect on the environment. Use it to keep up with new trends!

D globaleco.org
This site explores the importance of energy in our daily lives, and also different ways of generating it without using oil or gas, for example by using wind power instead. There are links to UK companies that use these renewable energies, so you can find out more about what they do.

E eco.org
Contact others who also care about environmental issues and find information about international groups; search for one to join in your area. You can also find out if your choice of transport damages the planet. If so, try the easy changes to your routine suggested here.

F planetmatters.org
Learn about what top scientists involved in research to protect our planet do day to day, as well as about their latest discoveries. There's a message board so you can post questions to them – you'll always get a quick reply. There's also a recycling section – find different uses for things that you might otherwise put in the bin.

G worldaware.org
Most people want to know what they can do to help protect our world. This site has everything you need to know about recycling: why it's important around the world, and how to get rid of items safely in your local area without harming the environment.

H oneworld.org
There's lots of environmental information here, whether you're just starting to explore the subject, or wanting to find out about the latest research. Gifts are on sale, too, made from objects and materials that are often thrown out – treat yourself and help the planet! There's also a useful guide on using less electricity at home – reduce those bills!

Part 3

Questions 11–15

For each question, choose the correct answer.

Basketball player

Luka Horvat writes about his early career.

My dad was a professional basketball player in Germany, as his father had been before him, and I went to watch many of his games when I was a kid. You might think that seeing so many matches would give me a love of the sport, but it actually had the opposite effect. I loved telling my friends how good my dad was, of course, especially when he won a game, but I used to take a book with me to read instead of watching.

Starting secondary school, I was still two years away from being a teenager but was already two metres tall. Seeing my height, my sports teacher asked if I'd be interested in training with the basketball team. Even though I enjoyed the session, I thought I'd need to develop my skills before I took part in a real match, but the teacher had more confidence in me than I did. It took me a while to agree, but a few weeks later I found myself playing against a team from another school. Mum and Dad coming to watch didn't really help – it made me more nervous. But it was OK in the end!

For the next four years, I practised every day and did really well, even joining an adult team before I moved abroad to a special sports academy in the USA when I was fifteen. The coach there trains Olympic basketball players, and it was fantastic to work with him. However, I can't say I enjoyed my first experience of living far from my parents. At home, I'd never been able to spend much time with my friends due to all the training, so that wasn't such a change for me. I got used to everything about my new life in the end, though, and my English improved quickly too!

I turned professional at the age of eighteen, three years after arriving in the USA. I'd been taller than most players in the professional league since I was fifteen, but had been much too light for my height, so had to get that right first. My coach already knew a team that would take me while I was still at college, so I joined them and have never regretted it.

11 What does Luka say about his childhood?

   A   He had a great interest in basketball.

   B   He enjoyed watching his father play basketball.

   C   He felt proud of his father's success at basketball.

   D   He knew he wanted to become a basketball player.

12 How did Luka feel before his first match at secondary school?

   A   He wasn't sure that he would do well.

   B   He was pleased that his parents would be there.

   C   He wasn't happy about his teacher's attitude.

   D   He was delighted to be part of the team.

13 Luka thinks the most difficult thing about moving to the USA was

   A   learning a new language.

   B   being away from his family.

   C   getting a good coach.

   D   missing his friends.

14 What did Luka have to do before he became a professional player?

   A   complete his studies

   B   find a suitable team

   C   reach a certain height

   D   put on weight

15 What would be a good way to introduce this article?

   A   Luka Horvat has always been as interested in reading as in basketball. Here, in his own words, he explains why.

   B   Luka Horvat tells us how he became the latest member of a sporting family to become a professional basketball player.

   C   Professional basketball player Luka Horvat explains how luck has been so much more important than hard work in his career.

   D   Even though he only started playing basketball as a teenager, Luka Horvat still managed to become a professional by the age of eighteen.

Part 4

Questions 16–20

Five sentences have been removed from the text below.
For each question, choose the correct answer.
There are three extra sentences which you do not need to use.

Adventures in the air

The first ever balloon flight carrying passengers was made by the Montgolfier brothers in 1783. They used hot air to float the balloon over 1,000 metres up into the sky. Nowadays, people still fly in hot-air balloons but there is also a less well-known sport called 'cluster ballooning'; instead of one big balloon, hundreds of small balloons are used.

Cluster ballooning was invented by a lorry driver called Larry Walters. Larry had wanted to fly using balloons for a long time. **16** ____ It took almost 20 years, however, for his dream to finally come true. One day, Larry decided to do an experiment: he wanted to try flying a few metres above his garden. So he bought 45 balloons, filled them with a gas called helium, and tied them to a chair. He then cut the rope that was holding the chair to the ground. **17** ____ The chair, with Larry sitting in it, floated several kilometres into the sky rather than just a few metres!

The wind was blowing strongly and Larry began to float out towards the sea. Things were getting dangerous. Then, to make matters even worse, the wind changed, and the balloons started to blow towards the local airport. Larry felt very worried. **18** ____ The story of Larry's flight was all over the news and this is how the adventure sport of cluster ballooning was born.

One experienced cluster balloonist, Leo Burns, flew his cluster balloons over the largest range of mountains in Europe – the Alps. This wasn't his first flight, though. Leo had got his pilot's licence several years before, so was already used to flying. **19** ____ According to Leo, there is no better way to fly. 'Cluster ballooning's amazing,' he says. 'The balloons are usually completely silent. **20** ____ They weren't as safe as modern cluster balloons either.'

A	He knew this would still make him feel very afraid.
B	The old-fashioned hot-air balloons made a horrible noise.
C	In fact, he was just a boy when he first started thinking about it.
D	Luckily, he landed safely after a couple of hours.
E	They are also much less dangerous.
F	However, there was an unexpected problem.
G	But these days, he prefers to use balloons.
H	Immediately after that, he tried to learn how this would be possible.

Part 5

Questions 21–26

For each question, choose the correct answer.

Whale songs

Did you know that a kind of whale, called a humpback whale, sings? In the 1960s it was **(21)** .... that humpbacks communicate with each other by making beautiful noises. A record was **(22)** .... in 1970 called *Songs of the humpback whale*, which sold millions of copies. People were absolutely amazed to learn that some whales in the deep oceans were so intelligent: in **(23)** .... centuries people had thought that whales had simple brains, like fish.

The songs of the whales were so popular that they were **(24)** .... in recordings of sounds from our planet which were **(25)** .... into space in 1977. The recordings were chosen to show the wide **(26)** .... of life on our planet. People hoped that, in the future, they might be found by intelligent creatures far out in space.

21	A	explored	B	invented	C	discovered	D	informed
22	A	appeared	B	delivered	C	achieved	D	produced
23	A	previous	B	old	C	early	D	ancient
24	A	contained	B	included	C	consisted	D	involved
25	A	sent	B	added	C	kept	D	placed
26	A	sort	B	difference	C	kind	D	variety

Part 6

Questions 27–32

For each question, write the correct answer.
Write **one** word for each gap.

My travel blog

This summer, I travelled to Copenhagen, the capital of Denmark, on my own. I am only 20 and to **(27)** .... honest, I was nervous about exploring a new city alone. I decided to go on a free walking tour the first day I was there. I hoped the tour would help me to become more familiar **(28)** .... the city.

Unfortunately, the weather wasn't great, but the tour was still absolutely fantastic! Magnus, our tour guide, knew all about the city's history. We also learnt loads **(29)** .... interesting facts about Danish culture. At the end of the tour, he gave **(30)** .... all suggestions for the best places **(31)** .... eat and visit.

Apart from learning so much, I actually had a lot more fun on the walking tour **(32)** .... I'd expected. It was an excellent way to experience the city, and learn about its culture and history.

Test 2

WRITING (45 minutes)

Part 1

You **must** answer this question.
Write your answer in about **100 words** on the answer sheet.

Question 1

Read this email from your English-speaking friend Robbie and the notes you have made.

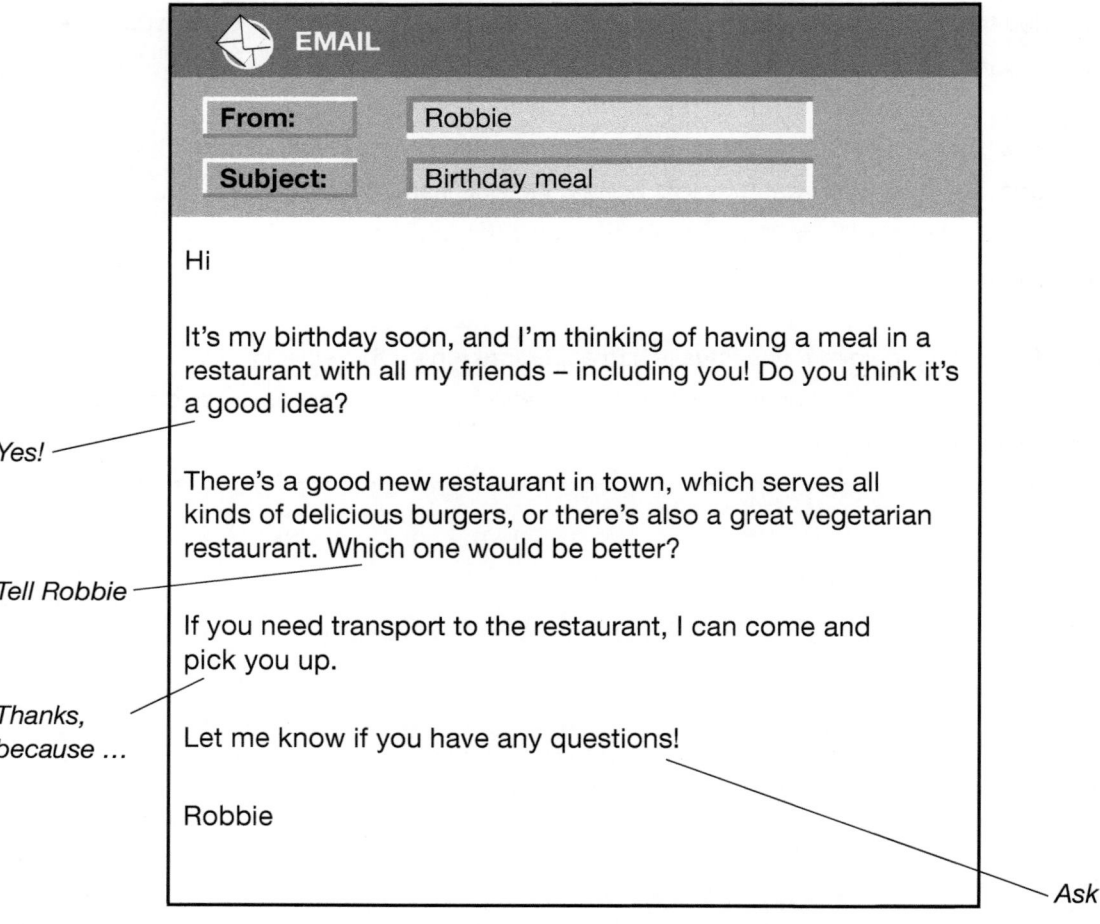

Write your **email** to Robbie using **all the notes**.

Part 2

Choose **one** of these questions.
Write your answer in about **100 words** on the answer sheet.

Question 2

You see this announcement on an English-language website.

Articles wanted!

Free-time activities

What activities can people your age do in their free time where you live?
Do you enjoy taking part in organised activities? Why?
Is there a new activity that you would like to be available in your area?

We'll publish the best articles answering these questions next month.

Write your **article**.

Question 3

Your English teacher has asked you to write a story.
Your story must begin with this sentence.

As I came out of the supermarket, I saw someone that I had wanted to see for a long time.

Write your **story**.

Test 2

LISTENING (approximately 30 minutes)

Part 1

Questions 1–7

For each question, choose the correct answer.

1 What has the man forgotten to pack for the trip?

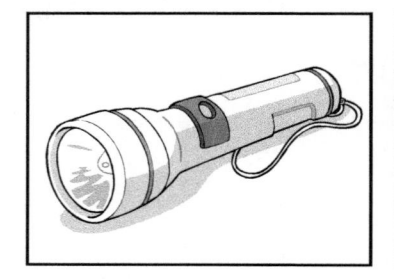

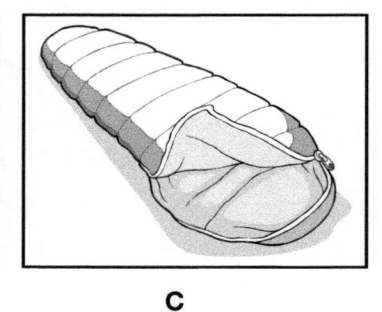

    A   B   C

2 What time is the plane expected to depart?

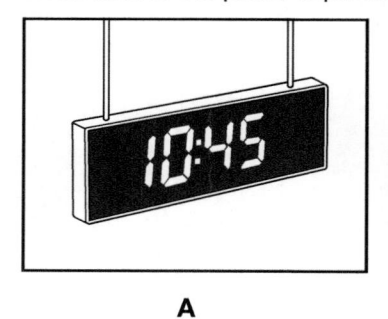

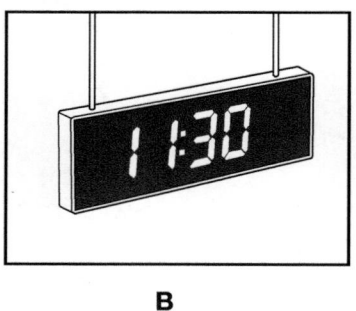

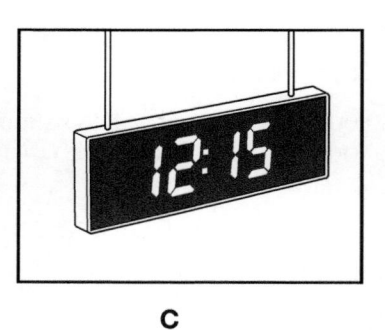

    A   B   C

3 Where did the family go at the weekend?

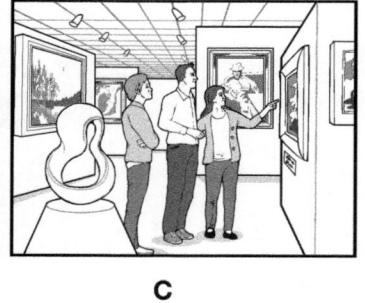

    A   B   C

38

Listening

4 What are the man and woman going to order?

A 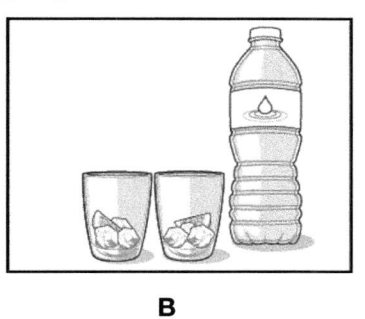   B    C

5 Which photograph did the man take?

A 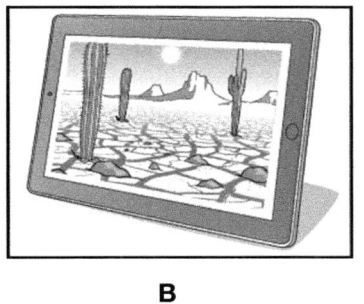   B 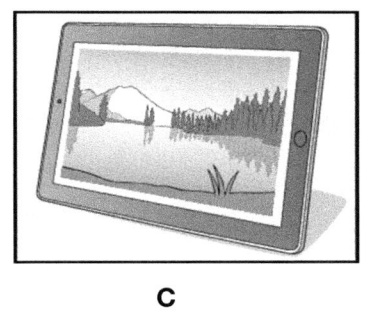   C

6 How does the man suggest his friends should travel to the concert?

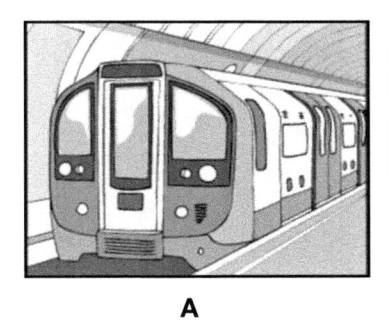

A    B    C

7 What is the weather forecast for the north this morning?

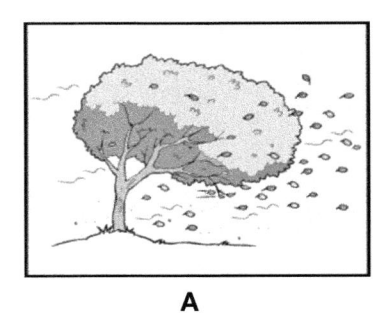

A    B    C

Test 2

Part 2

Questions 8–13

For each question, choose the correct answer.

---

8   You will hear a boy telling a friend about plans for his birthday.
    How does he feel about the plans he's made?

    A   annoyed that some of his friends don't want to come

    B   disappointed that he can't invite more friends

    C   worried that it might be boring for his friends

9   You will hear two friends talking about a football match they went to.
    They both think that

    A   the crowd was smaller than usual.

    B   the match was quite boring.

    C   the referee made some bad decisions.

10 You will hear a man telling his friend about a skiing holiday.
    How did he feel during the holiday?

    A   upset that he was injured

    B   embarrassed by his skiing ability

    C   angry that his friends put photos online

11 You will hear two friends talking about cars.
    The woman thinks the best way to get information about new cars is from

    A   advertisements.

    B   TV programmes.

    C   internet reviews.

Listening

12 You will hear a woman telling a friend about a singing competition.
    What does the woman say about it?

    A   Judging it is the easiest part.

    B   It is taking a long time to organise it.

    C   She would love to perform in it.

13 You will hear a woman talking to a friend about her recent move to a city.
    How does the woman feel about it?

    A   pleased about a surprising health benefit

    B   glad that she has met friendly people

    C   satisfied with her local area

Test 2

Part 3

Questions 14–19

For each question, write the correct answer in the gap. Write **one** or **two words** or a **number** or a **date** or a **time**.

You will hear a woman called Kelly Robinson talking about her work as a maker of cartoon films.

The maker of cartoon films

Kelly did a degree in **(14)** .... at university.

Kelly really enjoys going to work because of the **(15)** .... at the company.

Kelly's department is responsible for creating **(16)** .... in cartoons.

At the moment Kelly is trying to develop her **(17)** .... skills.

It takes Kelly's company **(18)** .... to make a full-length cartoon film.

Kelly's next project will be some cartoons for a **(19)** ....

Part 4

Questions 20–25

For each question, choose the correct answer.

You will hear an interview with a girl called Rosie Banks, who swims in international competitions.

20 Rosie swam a lot when she was very young because

    A her father thought it was an important skill.

    B she wanted to be like her brother.

    C there were free classes at her local pool.

21 What did Rosie dislike about doing serious swimming training?

    A being away from her friends

    B the long journey from home

    C missing some school lessons

22 When Rosie won the Swim Stars International competition she was

    A surprised by the public interest.

    B amazed that she had done so well.

    C excited about meeting other famous sportspeople.

23 Rosie says she needs more help with the cost of

    A transport to competitions.

    B the kit she needs.

    C her accommodation while she's abroad.

24 What has Rosie changed since she got a new coach?

    A her swimming style

    B what she eats

    C her fitness routine

25 What is Rosie planning to do in Spain?

    A take part in some races

    B train with different people

    C have some time to relax

Test 3

READING (45 minutes)

Part 1

Questions 1–5

For each question, choose the correct answer.

1

> Zara,
> Really sorry – I have to work late tonight so can't cook dinner after all. I know you're busy and your brother's coming round. Could you order a takeaway? I'll eat at work.
> Ali

Zara should

A buy something for Ali's dinner.

B have dinner without Ali.

C eat the dinner that Ali has made.

2

> **For sale**
> Traditional wooden dining table and chairs.
> Some damage to table top.
> Call Mark after 7 p.m. on
> 087322 51983

What does the seller say?

A The items he has got are not all in perfect condition.

B You can contact him any time you like.

C His furniture is not made in an old-fashioned style.

3

> This tennis equipment is for club members only.
> To hire rackets and balls for use on the court, see Reception.

A You're not permitted to use this equipment unless you have club membership.

B If you wish to become a member of the tennis club, ask at Reception.

C Non-members must bring their own equipment to use on these courts.

44

4

Aiden

I'm afraid I'm unwell – I can't go to the running club today. But you should definitely go, even though it's your first time. Everyone in the group's really helpful – especially if you're new.

Olivia

A Olivia is encouraging Aiden to go running today.

B Olivia wants Aiden to tell the group that she can't run today.

C Olivia is letting Aiden know that the running group are expecting him today.

5

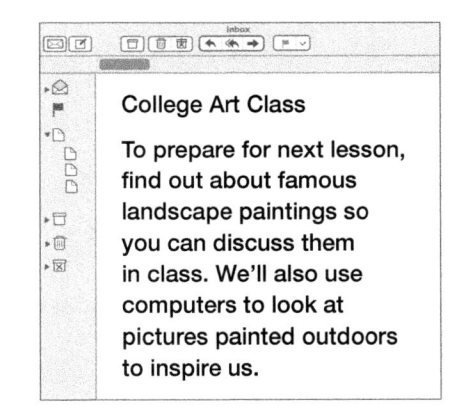

College Art Class

To prepare for next lesson, find out about famous landscape paintings so you can discuss them in class. We'll also use computers to look at pictures painted outdoors to inspire us.

A Students will be working outdoors during their next art class.

B Students must produce their next picture using painting software.

C Students should do some research before the next session.

Test 3

Part 2

Questions 6–10

For each question, choose the correct answer.

The people below all want to find a castle to visit.
On the opposite page there are descriptions of eight castles.
Decide which castle would be the most suitable for the people below.

6 Alan is keen on history, and wants to visit a castle that was the site of well-known historical events. He'd like the castle to be near the coast, with tours led by a guide.

7 Yoshiko wants to see a castle that people are still living in. She loves visiting beautiful gardens, and would like to explore interesting places in the castle.

8 Paulo and Maria collect antiques, so want to visit a castle that still has some of its original furniture on display, and hear about the building's history. They also want something that's particularly suitable for young children.

9 Kerim wants somewhere with a great historical atmosphere, with typical food from the past to try, and people dressed in costume. He'd also like to see art that's been in the castle for centuries.

10 Jake and his brother have always wanted to visit the ruins of a castle surrounded by water, with great views. Jake also wants to learn about any wildlife living in and around the castle.

Castles to visit

A **Durston Castle** has a valuable art collection, secret tunnels – one leading to the beach – and visitors mustn't miss the unusual rooms deep beneath the castle walls. Because the building is the Durston family's home, some parts cannot be visited – but you can sit on the grass under the trees and admire the flower beds and fountains. There's a play area for children too.

B At **Castle Woodward**, experience what life was like at the time it was built. Staff wear clothes typical of the time, and offer everyone tasty snacks made using recipes from different periods of history. Inside, the walls are covered with original paintings of the generations of people who've lived in the castle.

C **Castle Hemsworth**'s guides, dressed in historical costumes, give visitors information about the traditional castle building, towers and gardens. Wild horses live nearby. Inside, the castle looks unchanged, with old furniture and portraits of people who've lived here.

D Only a few parts of the ancient castle of **Marlin** are left, but you can still visit some underground rooms and see beautiful countryside from the high tower. The castle is in the middle of a lake and has lovely gardens. There are talks about the castle, and the bats, birds and butterflies that have made Marlin their home.

E **Chartsmouth Castle** was once owned and lived in by kings. Visitors love exploring the rooms, some of which have hidden tunnels. You can see the sea from the top of the walls, and younger visitors will love the outdoor games.

F Experts at the ruins of **Carston Castle** will show you around and give you information – and offer you 17th-century snacks! Hear how the building was once the scene of famous battles, and is now home to a variety of wildlife. And from the south side, there are fantastic sea views.

G **Rushford** is an old castle on the coast which is a popular local attraction. The Rushford Castle café in the walls serves food typical of the castle's history. Inside, there are beautiful rooms with antique tables and clocks. Outside, visitors can see a wide variety of wildlife.

H *Sawbridge Castle was built in 1712 on an island in a lake. Inside, you can still see beautifully designed beds, tables and other objects once used by families living there. Put on headphones and listen to information about the history of Sawbridge Castle. Visitors of all ages will love the toy museum in the gardens.*

Part 3

Questions 11–15

For each question, choose the correct answer.

Ana Ronson

Singer-songwriter

Singer-songwriter Ana Ronson grew up in Ireland. Although her parents weren't musicians, there was always music in the house. Her grandfather played the guitar, and taught Ana and her brother to play.

The first time Ana tried singing in front of an audience was at school – she was so nervous that her teacher had to lead her off the stage. This teacher suggested that joining the school theatre club might make her more confident. After attending the club for a while, she happily sang with 50 other students at an end-of-term concert.

A year later, her brother, who was in a band, asked her to write a song for them, and so she wrote her first ever song, *Falling Stars*. Writing it took just three days and she enjoyed it so much that she enrolled on a songwriting course run by a professional songwriter. Despite being the youngest student, she already knew more about music than many of the others. But Ana says the teacher didn't listen to anything she said, and she wrote *Something to Say* about how annoyed this made her feel.

She posted this song online, and it became a huge success. She was delighted when people left comments saying that they loved it and found new meanings in the words each time they heard them. Joss Alton, the owner of a recording company called Isotope Music, flew from his office on the other side of Ireland to ask her to join Isotope. At first she wasn't sure; she didn't know anything about the company, and didn't want someone telling her what to sing. However, Joss persuaded her this wouldn't happen, and a short time later she performed at a concert in Dublin arranged by Isotope. They sold all the tickets very quickly and it was an amazing evening.

Ana says she's less interested in writing songs about when life's good; when it's not, there's more for her to say. One of her favourite songs is *Decision*, written about why her brother stopped singing for a while, and how unhappy it made him. While she hopes that fans will like her songs, her aim is to write about personal experiences that matter to her.

11 What helped Ana stop being scared of singing to an audience?

  A practising her singing with a band
  B asking a teacher to stand on stage with her
  C being in a drama group at school
  D making sure she was not in the front row

12 How was the songwriting course useful for Ana?

  A She was able to meet some well-known singers.
  B The teacher's attitude gave her an idea for a song.
  C She learnt a lot from other writers on the course.
  D The teacher gave her advice about the music business.

13 Ana decided to work with Joss Alton because

  A he promised to let her choose which songs to sing.
  B he offered to help her put on a concert.
  C she liked some other singers that he worked with.
  D he owned a company in her home town.

14 Ana most enjoys writing songs that

  A she is sure her fans will like.
  B deal with difficult times.
  C her brother can sing with his band.
  D help people remember their own experiences.

15 What would Ana write to fans in her blog?

  A Listening to my parents playing music on their instruments really encouraged me to become a singer myself.

  B Writing songs just gets easier with practice. Nowadays it only takes a week or so – it wasn't like that when I started!

  C I loved playing the concert in Dublin. I hope that next time we'll sell all the tickets – it was a shame to have some empty seats!

  D I read what people write about me online – it means a lot to me that they like listening carefully to my songs.

Part 4

Questions 16–20

Five sentences have been removed from the text below.
For each question, choose the correct answer.
There are three extra sentences which you do not need to use.

Steve Dalway's cycle ride

Steve Dalway has recently completed an amazing bike ride between the US cities of Los Angeles and Boston, a distance of nearly 5,500 km. He and ten other cyclists took part in a trip organised by a company that provided a mechanic, planned the accommodation and route, and carried the cyclists' bags. **16** _____ Even with these, the ride involved a huge amount of effort.

Steve had already completed another long cycle ride in Europe. **17** _____ For example, he knew that on any ride, eating properly is important. When you don't eat enough, your ability to recover after hard exercise is reduced. For this reason, he always made sure he had a large breakfast before setting off every morning. **18** _____ The sight of the hotel at the end of the day was still very welcome, however!

One of the toughest times for the riders in the US was when the route climbed high into the Rocky Mountains. By the end of that part of the ride, Steve had climbed an amazing 28,000 m in total.

19 _____ An early section of the ride, for instance, took the group of cyclists through the Mojave desert, where the high temperatures made them feel as if they were in an oven. In the desert, Steve had to drink four litres of liquid every 40 km in order to keep going.

The cyclists used paper maps and had electronic devices to record the distances they travelled. So that everyone knew what they'd be facing the next day, a big map was displayed every evening in the hotel where the group were staying. **20** _____ At first the cyclists were disappointed when the black line drawn on the map by the organisers only moved forward by small amounts, despite all the day's work. At the end of the ride, however, they felt very proud of what they'd achieved.

A	He therefore had an idea of what to expect on this one.
B	It also allowed them to see the progress they had made.
C	He was surprised that he had gone so fast.
D	Doing that gave him the energy he needed to keep going.
E	It also arranged stops every 50 km for snacks and drinks.
F	This ride would be 1,000 km longer.
G	As a result, Steve's family knew how he was feeling each day.
H	There were other challenges, too.

Part 5

Questions 21–26

For each question, choose the correct answer.

Honey

People all over the world enjoy eating honey. But how much do you know about this **(21)** .... food? Most honey is made by bees, but what few people realise is that there are several types of bee which make honey.

Bees may have to visit about two million flowers to produce only half a kilo of honey. The type of flower the bees visit **(22)** .... both how the honey tastes and its colour. In fact, there are **(23)** .... more than three hundred kinds of honey.

In **(24)** .... times, honey was added to food instead of sugar, as sugar was very rare. In many cultures, people have used it for centuries to **(25)** .... various health problems. **(26)** ...., people all over the world still add it to hot water and drink it when they have a sore throat.

21	**A**	usual	**B**	shared	**C**	general	**D**	common
22	**A**	makes	**B**	affects	**C**	guides	**D**	directs
23	**A**	correctly	**B**	actually	**C**	accurately	**D**	absolutely
24	**A**	antique	**B**	far	**C**	elderly	**D**	ancient
25	**A**	cure	**B**	mend	**C**	repair	**D**	assist
26	**A**	Recently	**B**	Lately	**C**	Nowadays	**D**	Already

Part 6

Questions 27–32

For each question, write the correct answer.
Write **one** word for each gap.

Starting at college

Hi, my name's Emma. Welcome to the college! I've been studying here for a year now. Starting at college isn't easy, but I'm sure you'll soon feel at home. When I first started studying here last year, I was **(27)** .... nervous that I couldn't even ask anyone for help. I got lost five times on my first day!

Remember that **(28)** .... student at the college has been new at one time, and understands how you feel. So **(29)** .... you're not sure where to go, just ask – we're all happy to help!

You probably don't know many people here. To make some friends, **(30)** .... not spend break times with some of your new classmates in the café? Or how **(31)** .... joining one of the many clubs we have at the college? **(32)** .... are lots to choose from.

Good luck on your new course!

Test 3

WRITING (45 minutes)

Part 1

You **must** answer this question.
Write your answer in about **100 words** on the answer sheet.

Question 1

Read this email from your college English teacher Miss Jones and the notes you have made.

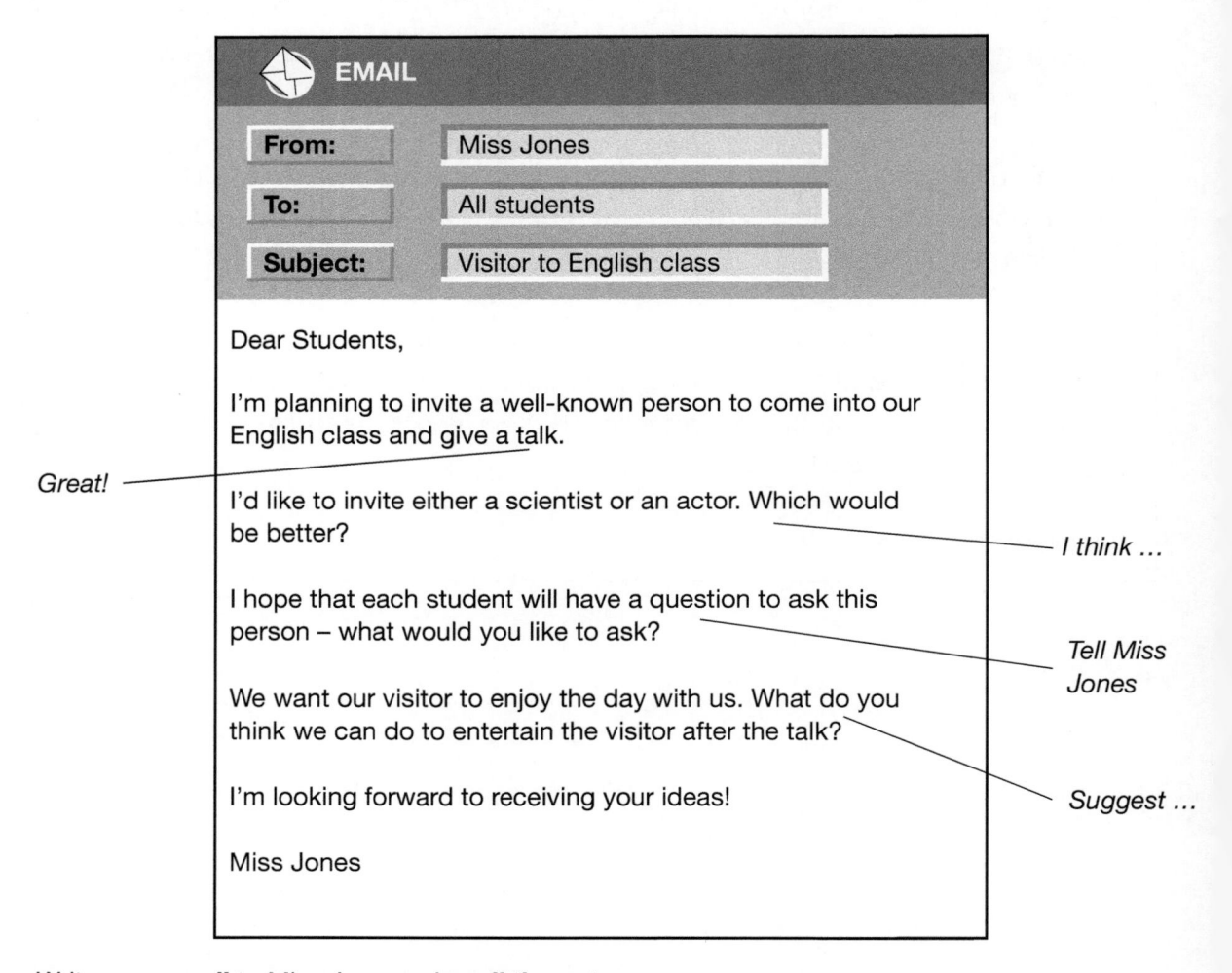

EMAIL

From: Miss Jones
To: All students
Subject: Visitor to English class

Dear Students,

I'm planning to invite a well-known person to come into our English class and give a talk. — *Great!*

I'd like to invite either a scientist or an actor. Which would be better? — *I think ...*

I hope that each student will have a question to ask this person – what would you like to ask? — *Tell Miss Jones*

We want our visitor to enjoy the day with us. What do you think we can do to entertain the visitor after the talk? — *Suggest ...*

I'm looking forward to receiving your ideas!

Miss Jones

Write your **email** to Miss Jones using **all the notes**.

Writing

Part 2

Choose **one** of these questions.
Write your answer in about **100 words** on the answer sheet.

Question 2

You see this announcement in an English-language magazine.

Articles wanted!

Computer games

Do you and your friends enjoy playing computer games?
What are the good and bad things about computer games?

The most interesting articles answering these questions will appear in our magazine.

Write your **article**.

Question 3

Your English teacher has asked you to write a story.
Your story must begin with this sentence.

It was my first time in the jungle and I was so excited.

Write your **story**.

Test 3

LISTENING (approximately 30 minutes)

Part 1

Questions 1–7

For each question, choose the correct answer.

1 Why was the man late?

A   B   C

2 Why is the main road closed today?

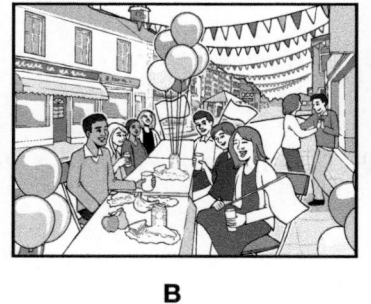

A   B   C

3 Where do they decide to have the wedding anniversary party?

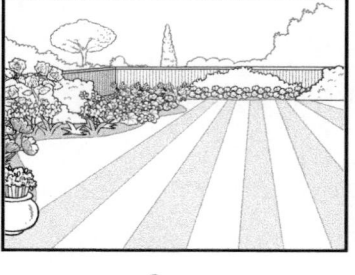

A   B   C

56

Listening

4 What does the man decide to order?

A   B   C

5 Which armchair is the man going to buy?

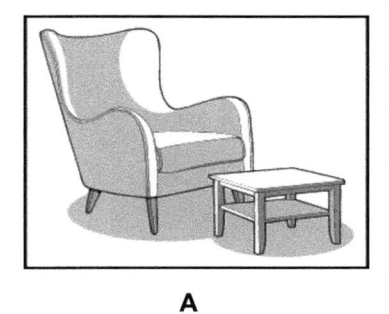

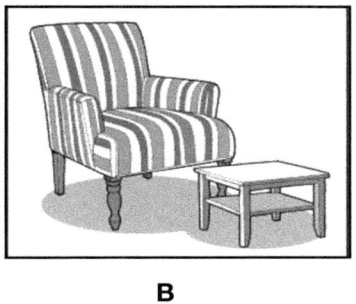

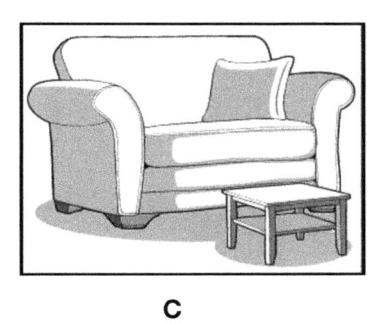

A   B   C

6 Which concert has the woman arranged to attend?

A   B   C

7 Which tomatoes will the man use?

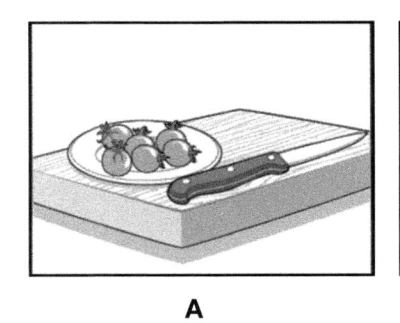

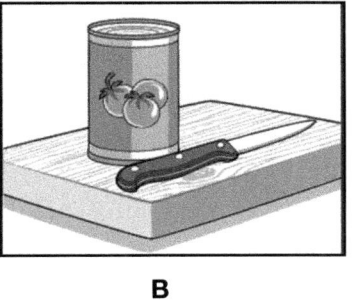

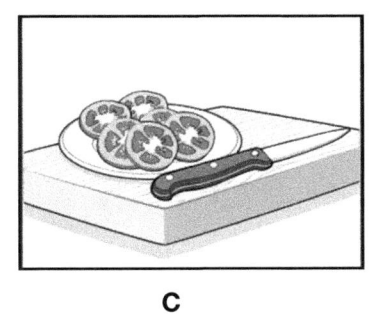

A   B   C

Test 3

Part 2

Questions 8–13

For each question, choose the correct answer.

---

8   You will hear two friends talking about doing exercise.
    Why is the man finding it difficult to do exercise?

    A   He can't afford to go to the gym.

    B   He doesn't have a lot of free time.

    C   There aren't any sports facilities nearby.

9   You will hear two people talking in a restaurant.
    They agree that

    A   the soup was very spicy.

    B   the fish dishes were very tasty.

    C   one of the desserts was very small.

10 You will hear a woman telling her friend about her neighbours.
    What problem does she have with her neighbours?

    A   They are noisy.

    B   They are unfriendly.

    C   They are untidy.

11 You will hear two friends talking about a new museum.
    What does the woman say about it?

    A   She was surprised by some things on display.

    B   The opening hours suit her.

    C   She hopes to have another chance to visit.

Listening

12 You will hear a man talking to a colleague about a hotel he stayed in.
He complains that

   A   the room was too small for him.

   B   the location wasn't what he expected.

   C   he was disturbed by the traffic.

13 You will hear two passengers talking on an aeroplane.
How does the woman feel about flying?

   A   She thinks it's very convenient.

   B   She finds it a relaxing way to travel.

   C   She prefers travelling by train to flying.

Part 3

Questions 14–19

For each question, write the correct answer in the gap. Write **one** or **two words** or a **number** or a **date** or a **time**.

You will hear a tour guide talking about arrangements for a day trip to a place called Gulum.

Day trip to Gulum

Bus leaves at: **(14)** ……………… a.m.

Meet before trip at: hotel **(15)** ………………

First stop: ruin of a **(16)** ………………

Lunch at: The **(17)** ……………… Restaurant

Afternoon activity: **(18)** ……………… or beach volleyball

Bring: **(19)** ………………

Part 4

Questions 20–25

For each question, choose the correct answer.

You will hear an interview with a man called James Sweeney who works as a tree-climbing instructor.

20 How did James become interested in trees?

    A   He worked for someone who looked after trees.

    B   He enjoyed playing in trees when he was a child.

    C   He learnt about trees from his mother.

21 What surprised James when he first learnt to climb trees?

    A   the time it took to become good at it

    B   the wide range of people in the class

    C   the amount of equipment needed

22 What does James enjoy most about his teaching work?

    A   helping people who need the skill for their work

    B   giving people an interesting new experience

    C   showing people how to climb in different kinds of weather

23 James travels around the USA a lot because

    A   interest in tree climbing is increasing there.

    B   there isn't much work in his own area in winter.

    C   he'd like to visit as many parts of the country as possible.

24 What does James like about sleeping in trees?

    A   He wakes up to the sound of birds.

    B   He thinks it's comfortable.

    C   He can look at the stars.

25 When James climbs in the rainforests, he moves more slowly because

    A   he wants to study the insects.

    B   he finds the trees difficult to climb.

    C   he has to protect the trees.

Test 4

READING (45 minutes)

Part 1

Questions 1–5

For each question, choose the correct answer.

1

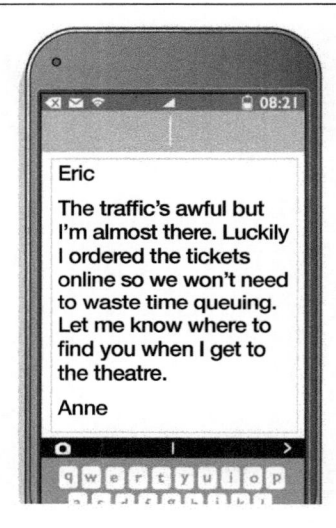

Eric

The traffic's awful but I'm almost there. Luckily I ordered the tickets online so we won't need to waste time queuing. Let me know where to find you when I get to the theatre.

Anne

Why is Anne texting?

A to ask Eric if he can do her a favour

B to remind Eric about what they have agreed

C to give Eric an update regarding their arrangement

2

Final-year Students

Ex-students from our course are coming here next week to talk to you about how to do well in your first job. Space for a maximum of thirty students, so sign up now.

A Students of any year group are able to come to the careers talk.

B Students should go to the talk if they need help applying for a job.

C Students must register quickly because places at the event are limited.

3

Recycling Centre Users

Glass, plastic and metal items must be cleaned before you bring them to the recycling centre. Please place them in the correct recycling bin – the recycling centre staff are there to help.

A Recycling centre staff will clean items for recycling.

B Certain items need to be washed before they are recycled.

C All items can be placed in the same recycling bin.

4

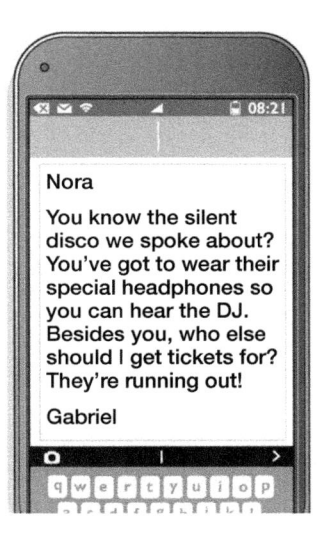

Nora

You know the silent disco we spoke about? You've got to wear their special headphones so you can hear the DJ. Besides you, who else should I get tickets for? They're running out!

Gabriel

A Gabriel has got a ticket for Nora to go to the special dance event.

B Gabriel is informing Nora that she needs to remember to bring headphones.

C Gabriel wants Nora to suggest who may be interested in going to the disco.

5

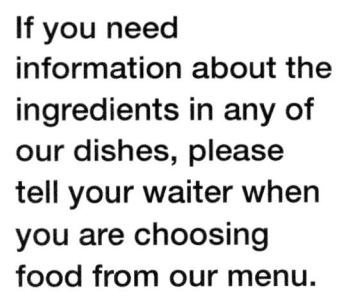

If you need information about the ingredients in any of our dishes, please tell your waiter when you are choosing food from our menu.

A Our staff can let you know about what we've used to make our dishes.

B Read the information on our menu if you need to avoid eating certain ingredients.

C Tell your waiter if you'd prefer something different from what's on the menu.

Part 2

Questions 6–10

For each question, choose the correct answer.

The people below all want to see a musical show at the theatre.
On the opposite page there are eight reviews of shows.
Decide which show would be the most suitable for the people below.

6 Erika wants to see a show with music and which has famous actors in the lead roles. She'd like it to be based on a book and contain many different types of music.

7 Guillermo would like to go to a show that's funny and is about a real person. He's looking for one with some music in it, but with more speaking than singing.

8 Neelam wants to see a musical show which contains lots of special effects and would like to watch it in an unusual place. She'd like to see a love story.

9 Oumar wants to go to a show that's a bit frightening. He'd like to see a story set in the past and realistic costumes from the period.

10 Mira wants a show with dancing, as well as songs by well-known musicians. She'd like the music to be in a range of styles from around the world.

The best musical shows in town

A Glad!
Glad! tells the story of a teenage girl whose dreams of becoming a famous musician come true with the help of some special (and amusing!) friends. The costumes and songs are amazing, and although it's fiction, it has the feel of a real-life story. It's on for one week only, on a temporary stage in the football stadium.

B Mary Wright
The two well-known lead actors in this 16th-century drama are surprisingly good dancers, and the music creates quite a scary atmosphere. The clothes by top designer Jean-Luc Filbert are historically accurate and look absolutely wonderful.

C The Amazing Mr Mason
This unusual musical is based on a famous story written over 400 years ago. The hero falls in love with a princess who's forced to move to another country. There's quite a lot of speaking for a musical, but the ending's a surprising pleasure.

D The End of Summer
You've probably read the novel which this musical comedy takes its story from, but you won't recognise the songs, as they were specially written for the show. Several songwriters were needed, due to the wide variety of music the producers wanted. The stars, who you'll probably recognise from TV, are fantastic.

E Keeping Time
Keeping Time is based on the real-life story of the popular group *Marcellous*, and includes their best work. We see how having members from three different continents allowed them to create songs using music from each place. Unusually, there's ballet in this show, but it goes surprisingly well with their music.

F No Exit
With its use of film and advanced technology to make it seem like the characters appear in two places at once, this spectacular musical starts off as an old-fashioned ghost story but quickly turns into a highly entertaining romantic comedy. The fact that the show is performed in an old factory building only adds to the enjoyment.

G Tiger Prince
The Tiger Prince leaves his jungle home and comes to the city in this fabulous musical. The story isn't particularly original but the computer-controlled light show goes perfectly with the amazing dance routines to make this a must-see show.

H The Final Whistle
If you're tired of serious dramas and dull love stories, why not give this laugh-a-minute show a try? The true story of basketball player Andy Hammond is cleverly told. Despite being advertised as a musical show, it actually has very few songs. You'll love all the brilliant jokes and entertaining conversations.

Part 3

Questions 11–15

For each question, choose the correct answer.

My Canadian trip

by Louise Walton

Last year I went on an amazing trip – travelling by boat on a guided group tour along the west coast of Canada. It was my brother Harry's idea. He's a journalist, like me, and he wanted to write articles about the trip. He's also a great fan of boats, although that's one interest we definitely don't share. But I'd dreamt of visiting the area ever since seeing it on TV as a child, especially as I knew it was where our great-grandparents had lived before moving to Europe. So I kept asking Harry if I could go too – until he finally agreed!

A few weeks before we left home, there were storms in the area we were going to. But luckily the forecast for the time we intended to be there was for calm seas. Although there was plenty to arrange, I was busy at work so didn't have much time to think about what needed doing. But Harry promised he'd taken care of everything, so I knew everything would be all right.

After arriving in Canada, we joined the group, packed our limited supplies into small boats and set off. The guide had mentioned that very few people now lived along that coast, and sure enough, the only other living creatures we saw for the first few days were dolphins and birds. We knew there were islands in the distance, but the early-morning fog made it hard to see very far, so I just focussed on the beautiful patterns our boat made in the water.

We often stopped for hours to explore the rock pools on the beaches. They were full of amazing coloured fish, many of which I didn't recognise. And it was great to be able to stop caring about how quickly or slowly the day was passing. We never forgot lunch or dinner, though, which we all made together over camp fires. When we finally fell asleep on the boats each evening, even though the beds were hard, it really felt like stress-free living!

When the time came to leave, I was sad. How could I return to normal life again? But I knew if I stayed, I'd miss family and friends. I was also looking forward to telling everyone at home about our adventures!

Reading

11 Why was Louise keen to go on the trip to Canada?

    A She liked the idea of spending time in a boat.

    B She knew her brother wanted her to accompany him.

    C She had wanted to travel there for a long time.

    D She had heard from some relatives who lived there.

12 Just before their departure, Louise

    A began to wonder how they would deal with bad weather.

    B was confident that they were fully prepared for the trip.

    C wished she could help her brother more.

    D felt she was better organised than usual.

13 On the first morning of the trip, Louise says she admired

    A the way the sea around them looked.

    B the wildlife which their boats attracted.

    C the homes that people had built in the area.

    D the views of islands they were passing.

14 During the trip, Louise enjoyed

    A learning the names of the fish she saw.

    B not having to cook regular meals.

    C spending the nights in comfort.

    D not having to worry about time.

15 What would Louise write in her diary during the trip?

A	There are wonderful pools along the coast, left behind by the sea. I wish we had the time to look at them more carefully.	**B**	I can't believe I'm in the same place I saw on that programme ages ago. Our great-grandparents would be amazed!
C	We've brought a lot of stuff with us in the boats – I'm sure it's not all necessary. It's surprising they don't sink!	**D**	It'll be hard to say goodbye to the place at the end, but I can't wait to get back to work – I've really missed it.

Part 4

Questions 16–20

Five sentences have been removed from the text below.
For each question, choose the correct answer.
There are three extra sentences which you do not need to use.

The Museum of Trash

In an industrial area in California, in the USA, large garbage trucks regularly deliver tons of rubbish to a recycling centre. Meanwhile, coaches deliver crowds of people who are coming to visit *The Museum of Trash*. **16** [   ] It is a colourful elephant made entirely out of rubbish.

The unusual sculpture was created out of all sorts of rubbish: old signs, mobile phones, shoes, sunglasses, plastic toys, car number plates, and anything else that the artist could get his hands on.

17 [   ] They have fun trying to find them all. The sculpture is 4 metres tall and weighs around 900 kg, which is equal to the average amount of rubbish each person in California throws away every year. **18** [   ]

While the elephant sculpture is popular, visitors also enjoy being able to see what happens at a real recycling centre. Rubbish which can be recycled is brought here every day. **19** [   ] People who live in these places are happy to know that what they throw away will not be wasted. Once it has arrived at the recycling centre, the rubbish is put into separate containers according to what it is made from, and sold to businesses that can use it to create new products. The companies make a range of things out of the recycled materials, and some of them can be bought in the museum shop.

'What is really exciting is that people go home and tell their friends what they can recycle,' says the museum's director. '**20** [   ] They can see where all the rubbish goes and learn that recycling is better than just wasting things.'

A	Few of these items were recycled into anything that people could wear.
B	Visitors are given a list of the different objects in it.
C	Although this might not seem like a lot, it is more than in most museums.
D	So while it is fun for visitors, they also pass on their new knowledge.
E	It comes from twenty towns in the local area.
F	Nowadays, however, over 30,000 visitors come to the museum each year.
G	The first display they see looks like something out of an animated movie.
H	It is certainly shocking to see what that actually looks like.

Test 4

Part 5

Questions 21–26

For each question, choose the correct answer.

Inventing the telephone

The telephone was invented by Alexander Graham Bell. His first career involved teaching people how to use a system which his father had **(21)** .... to help deaf people communicate. Because of this, Bell became more and more interested in all types of communication.

Bell wanted to **(22)** .... it possible for people to talk to each other over **(23)** .... distances. He realised that he had to turn sound into electricity and then back to sound again. This was a big engineering **(24)** ....

In 1876, after several months of hard work on this problem, Bell and his assistant Thomas Watson **(25)** .... it.

The first words ever spoken on the telephone are famous. Bell was working on their new invention in his laboratory when he accidentally **(26)** .... dangerous liquid on his clothes. He called Watson and said, 'Come here, I want to see you!'

21	A	thought	B	developed	C	done	D	reached
22	A	create	B	have	C	get	D	make
23	A	long	B	high	C	wide	D	far
24	A	request	B	demand	C	challenge	D	method
25	A	solved	B	answered	C	succeeded	D	found
26	A	lost	B	kept	C	fell	D	spilt

Part 6

Questions 27–32

For each question, write the correct answer.
Write **one** word for each gap.

From: Harry

To: Oliver

Subject: Piano lessons

Hi Oliver,

Guess what? I've finally started piano lessons, like you! As you know, it's something I've wanted to do ever **(27)** .... I was young. Anyway, a couple of months ago I saw someone playing the piano on TV – he was brilliant. And when I found out he'd only started playing quite recently, that encouraged **(28)** .... to start lessons.

I've got a really good teacher, and I go to her house twice a week **(29)** .... lessons. She's very patient. Every time I make a mistake, she explains what I did wrong. Also, I couldn't read music when I started. It's been hard to learn to read the notes on the page and decide which piano keys to use at the **(30)** .... time! But when I finally play something that other people recognise, it really makes me happy. Maybe **(31)** .... day, I'll become even better **(32)** .... you are at playing the piano!

Test 4

WRITING (45 minutes)

Part 1

You **must** answer this question.
Write your answer in about **100 words** on the answer sheet.

Question 1

Read this email from your English-speaking friend Jo and the notes you have made.

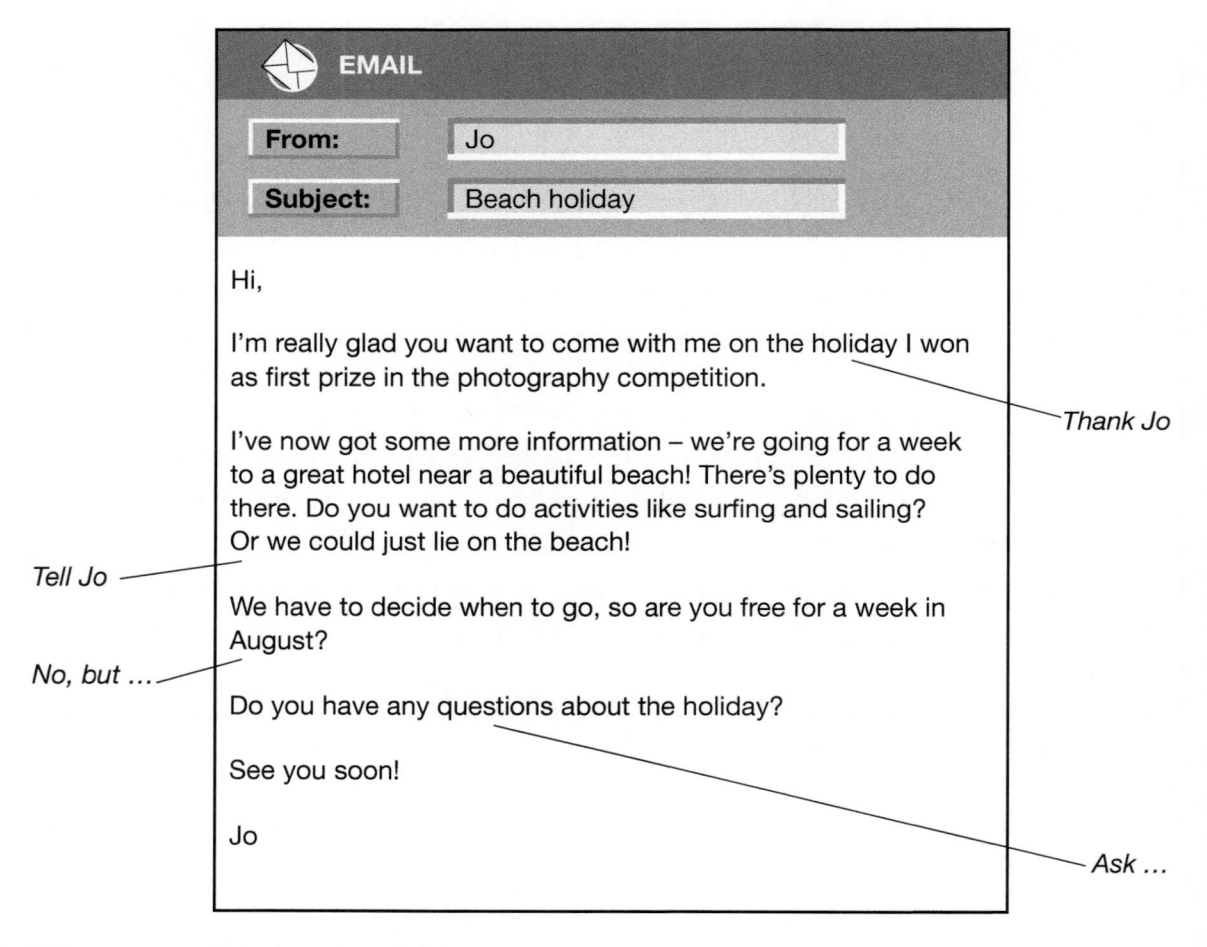

EMAIL

From: Jo
Subject: Beach holiday

Hi,

I'm really glad you want to come with me on the holiday I won as first prize in the photography competition. ← *Thank Jo*

I've now got some more information – we're going for a week to a great hotel near a beautiful beach! There's plenty to do there. Do you want to do activities like surfing and sailing? Or we could just lie on the beach! ← *Tell Jo*

We have to decide when to go, so are you free for a week in August? ← *No, but ...*

Do you have any questions about the holiday? ← *Ask ...*

See you soon!

Jo

Write your **email** to Jo using **all the notes**.

72

Part 2

Choose **one** of these questions.
Write your answer in about **100 words** on the answer sheet.

Question 2

You see this announcement in an English-language magazine.

Articles wanted!

Learning languages

Do you think it's important to learn a foreign language?
Is it better to learn a language in a group or on your own? Why?

We'll publish the most interesting articles answering these questions in our magazine.

Write your **article**.

Question 3

Your English teacher has asked you to write a story.
Your story must begin with this sentence.

The friends got off the bus and ran over to join the long queue of people.

Write your **story**.

Test 4

LISTENING (approximately 30 minutes)

Part 1

Questions 1–7

For each question, choose the correct answer.

1   How will the man travel to the city centre?

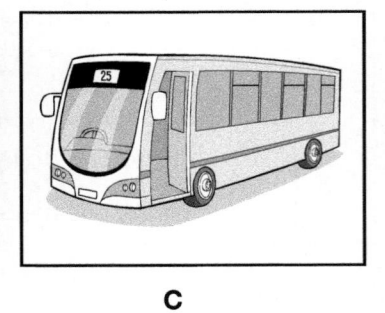

   A   B   C

2   What did the girl dislike at the hostel she stayed in?

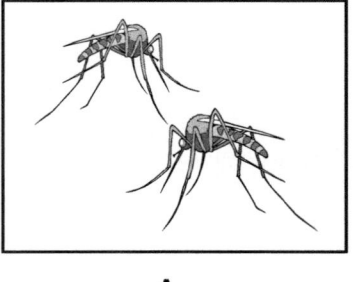

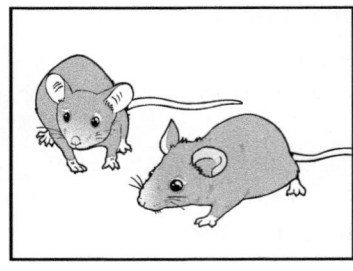

   A   B   C

3   What is the man going to order for lunch?

   A   B   C

74

Listening

4 What sport would the woman like to try?

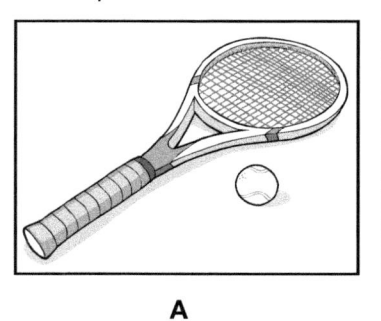

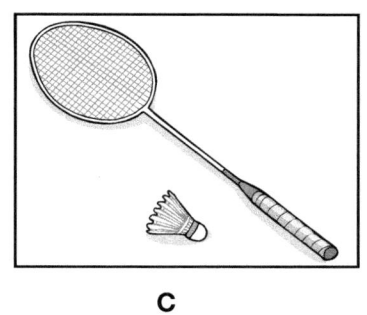

A B C

5 Which book is the man reading?

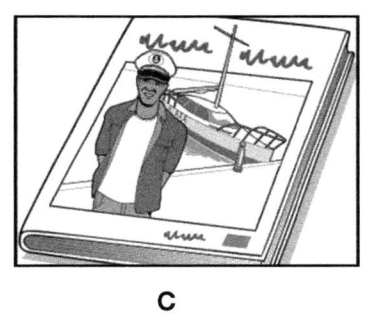

A B C

6 Where does the man suggest going at the weekend?

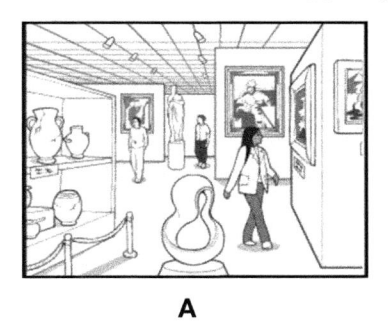

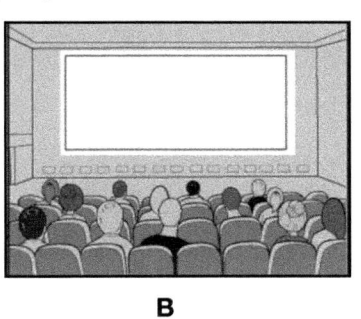

A B C

7 How much is the latest smartphone in the store today?

A B C

Test 4

Part 2

Questions 8–13

For each question, choose the correct answer.

---

8   You will hear a brother and sister talking about a gift for their cousin.
    Why do they decide to buy the gift online?

    A   It's heavy to carry home from the shop.

    B   It's not available in the shop.

    C   It's difficult to get to the shop.

9   You will hear two colleagues discussing their holiday travel plans.
    The man thinks that the woman should

    A   go somewhere new for her holiday.

    B   spend more time away.

    C   take a different type of transport.

10 You will hear a man talking to a friend about a fitness training session.
    The man cannot attend today's session because

    A   his doctor has advised him to rest.

    B   he has not recovered from a cold yet.

    C   he has just had an operation.

11 You will hear two friends talking about a play they've just seen.
    What does the woman say about the play?

    A   It improved after the interval.

    B   The costumes were strange.

    C   The acting was disappointing.

Listening

12 You will hear two friends talking about a film and its soundtrack.
What does the woman say about the soundtrack?

    A It's enjoyable for all ages.

    B It's relaxing to listen to.

    C It's better than the film.

13 You will hear two friends talking about the news.
They agree that

    A reading the news is an essential part of the day.

    B it's best to read the news online.

    C there's too much news about famous people.

Test 4

Part 3

Questions 14–19

For each question, write the correct answer in the gap. Write **one** or **two words** or a **number** or a **date** or a **time**.

You will hear a guide giving some information about a walk in the countryside.

Countryside walk

The walk will take **(14)** .... hours.

Walkers should be careful of **(15)** .... along the route.

Walkers will have lunch near the **(16)** ....

Walkers are likely to see wildlife including **(17)** ....

At the end of the walk, people can visit a **(18)** ....

It's possible to take a **(19)** .... back to the place where the walk started.

Listening

Part 4

Questions 20–25

For each question, choose the correct answer.

You will hear an interview with a young poet called Laura Dickson.

20 Laura first became interested in poetry

    A by reading it at home.

    B by studying it at school.

    C by learning about it from her father.

21 What made Laura decide to become a professional poet?

    A She met a famous poet.

    B She did a poetry course.

    C She won a poetry prize.

22 What is Laura's new book about?

    A various types of buildings

    B personal relationships

    C climate change

23 What does Laura say about reading poetry written a long time ago?

    A She admires how well it's written.

    B She finds it difficult to understand.

    C She prefers to read modern poems.

24 How does Laura feel about her new job teaching at a university?

    A pleased with her ability to do it well

    B grateful to have helpful colleagues

    C surprised by the amount of work

25 In the future, Laura would like to

    A organise a poetry festival.

    B take a break from writing poetry.

    C add music to some of her poetry.

Sample answer sheet: Reading

OFFICE USE ONLY - DO NOT WRITE OR MAKE ANY MARK ABOVE THIS LINE Page 1 of 2

Cambridge Assessment English

Candidate Name		Candidate Number	
Centre Name		Centre Number	
Examination Title		Examination Details	
Candidate Signature		Assessment Date	

Supervisor: If the candidate is ABSENT or has WITHDRAWN shade here ○

Preliminary Reading Candidate Answer Sheet

Instructions
Use a PENCIL (B or HB)
Rub out any answer you want to change with an eraser.

For Parts 1, 2, 3, 4 and 5:
Mark ONE letter for each answer.
For example: If you think A is the right answer to the question, mark your answer sheet like this: 0 [A] [B] [C]

Part 1
1 A B C
2 A B C
3 A B C
4 A B C
5 A B C

Part 2
6 A B C D E F G H
7 A B C D E F G H
8 A B C D E F G H
9 A B C D E F G H
10 A B C D E F G H

Part 3
11 A B C D
12 A B C D
13 A B C D
14 A B C D
15 A B C D

Part 4
16 A B C D E F G H
17 A B C D E F G H
18 A B C D E F G H
19 A B C D E F G H
20 A B C D E F G H

Part 5
21 A B C D
22 A B C D
23 A B C D
24 A B C D
25 A B C D
26 A B C D

Continues over ➡

OFFICE USE ONLY - DO NOT WRITE OR MAKE ANY MARK BELOW THIS LINE   Page 1 of 2

© UCLES 2019 Photocopiable

Sample answer sheet: Reading

OFFICE USE ONLY - DO NOT WRITE OR MAKE ANY MARK ABOVE THIS LINE   Page 2 of 2

For Part 6:
Write your answers clearly in the spaces next to the numbers (27 to 32) like this: `0 ENGLISH`

Write your answers in CAPITAL LETTERS.

Part 6	
27	
28	
29	
30	
31	
32	

Sample answer sheet: Writing 1

You must write within the grey lines.

Write your answer for Part 1 below. Do not write on the barcodes.

Question 1

This section for use by Examiner only:

C	CA	O	L

Sample answer sheet: Writing 2

You must write within the grey lines.

Answer only one of the two questions for Part 2.
Tick the box to show which question you have answered.
Write your answer below. Do not write on the barcodes.

Part 2	Question 2		Question 3	

This section for use by Examiner only:

C	CA	O	L

Sample answer sheet: Listening

OFFICE USE ONLY - DO NOT WRITE OR MAKE ANY MARK ABOVE THIS LINE — Page 1 of 1

Cambridge Assessment English

- Candidate Name
- Centre Name
- Examination Title
- Candidate Signature
- Candidate Number
- Centre Number
- Examination Details
- Assessment Date

Supervisor: If the candidate is ABSENT or has WITHDRAWN shade here ○

Preliminary Listening Candidate Answer Sheet

Instructions
Use a **PENCIL (B or HB)**. Rub out any answer you want to change with an eraser.

For Parts 1, 2 and 4:
Mark one letter for each answer. For example: If you think **A** is the right answer to the question, mark your answer sheet like this:

For Part 3:
Write your answers clearly in the spaces next to the numbers (14 to 19) like this:

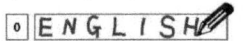

| 0 | E N G L I S H |

Write your answers in CAPITAL LETTERS.

Part 1
1. A B C
2. A B C
3. A B C
4. A B C
5. A B C
6. A B C
7. A B C

Part 2
8. A B C
9. A B C
10. A B C
11. A B C
12. A B C
13. A B C

Part 3
14. _____
15. _____
16. _____
17. _____
18. _____
19. _____

Part 4
20. A B C
21. A B C
22. A B C
23. A B C
24. A B C
25. A B C

OFFICE USE ONLY - DO NOT WRITE OR MAKE ANY MARK BELOW THIS LINE — Page 1 of 1

© UCLES 2019 Photocopiable

Acknowledgements

The authors and publishers acknowledge the following sources of copyright material and are grateful for the permissions granted. While every effort has been made, it has not always been possible to identify the sources of all the material used, or to trace all copyright holders. If any omissions are brought to our notice, we will be happy to include the appropriate acknowledgements on reprinting and in the next update to the digital edition, as applicable.

Photographs

Key: T = Test, R = Reading, ST = Speaking Test, P = Part.

All the photographs are sourced from Getty Images.

T1 R P2: Granger Wootz/Blend Images; Javier Sánchez Mingorance / EyeEm; Flashpop/DigitalVision; Indeed; rubberball; **T2 R P2:** LeoPatrizi/iStock/Getty Images Plus; Jason Todd/The Image Bank; Westend61; Compassionate Eye Foundation/DigitalVision; Calvin Dolley/Photographer's Choice; **T3 R P2:** Easy Production/ Cultura; BLOOMimage; theboone/E+; Gregory Costanzo/DigitalVision; Lena Koller/Johner Images; **T4 R P2:** Peter Widmann/EyeEm; Juanmonino/E+; Klaus Vedfelt/Taxi; AntonioGuillem/iStock/Getty Images Plus; Kay Fochtmann/EyeEm; **T1 ST:** Hero Images; Eugenio Marongiu/Cultura; **T2 ST:** Maskot; Pat Canova/Photolibrary; **T3 ST:** Astronaut Images/Caiaimage; Hero Images; **T4 ST:** BJI/Lane Oatey; SolStock/E+.

Typeset by QBS Learning.

Audio production by Real Deal Productions and dsound recording Ltd.

Visual materials for the Speaking test

Test 1

Part 2

Task 1A

Task 1B

Visual materials for the Speaking test

Test 1

Part 3

Task 1C

Choosing a book about interesting people

Visual materials for the Speaking test

Test 2

Part 2

Task 2A

Task 2B

Visual materials for the Speaking test

Test 2

Part 3

Task 2C

A present to take to a cold country

Visual materials for the Speaking test

Test 3

Part 2

Task 3A

Task 3B

Visual materials for the Speaking test

Test 3

Part 3

Task 3C

Using an empty building

Visual materials for the Speaking test

Test 4

Part 2

Task 4A

Task 4B

Visual materials for the Speaking test

Test 4

Part 3

Task 4C

Helping the environment

SPOT THE DIFFERENCE

That's right – there is no difference.

All our authentic practice tests go through the same design process as the official exam. We check every single part of our practice tests with real students under exam conditions, to make sure we give you the most authentic experience possible.

The official practice tests from Cambridge.